Living for Kicks

Jim McCarthy
& Kevin Cross

a mods graphic novel

OMNIBUS PRESS

London / New York / Paris / Sydney / Copenhagen / Berlin / Madrid / Tokyo

Living for Kicks

Jim McCarthy & Kevin Cross

a mods graphic novel

Copyright © 2016 Omnibus Press
(A Division of Music Sales Limited)

Cover illustrated by Kevin Cross
Text by Jim McCarthy
Book illustrated by Kevin Cross

ISBN: 978.1.78305.578.4
Order No: OP55902

Exclusive Distributors
Music Sales Limited,
14-15 Berners Street,
London, W1T 3LJ.

Music Sales Pty Ltd,
Australia and New Zealand,
Level 4, 30-32 Carrington Street,
Sydney NSW 2000,
Australia.

Every effort has been made to trace the copyright holders of the photographs in this
book but one or two were unreachable. We would be grateful if the photographers
concerned would contact us.

Printed in the EU.

A catalogue record for this book is available from the British Library.

Visit Omnibus Press on the web at **www.omnibuspress.com**

mods, skins, Sta-Prest, tonics and stuff...
reflections on mods

Living for Kicks came from a great initial idea which arose during a conversation with my managing editor, David Barraclough. We agreed the early sixties world of the mods was a perfect background for a graphic novel. The first thing I did was watch *Quadrophenia*, which I remembered as a pretty good film but hadn't seen for well over 20 years. I was determined not to copy the plot, either consciously or otherwise, but quickly realised that the mods and rockers skirmishes had to be included. However, I could not hang an entire book around that brief period, despite the hype it received during its fleeting heyday.

I liked *Quadrophenia* (sort of) when I rewatched it, mostly for the colloquial lingo and the huge amount of swearing. The plot and the film's third act, much less so. The story seemed to go off the boil and Phil Daniels' character (although well acted) just petered out.

I loved writing this story, especially with it being set in pre-PC times. It made me realise just how stultifying our present day culture can be. I can still remember the amount of slang and swearing around in the second half of the sixties when I was growing up. This was just after the mod period, when it had morphed into a skinhead culture (if I can use such a 'poncey' word as 'culture').

The clothes were still sharp, with Levi jeans and Levi Sta-Prest both very prevalent. Tonic suits, Prince of Wales checks, Harrington jackets and Ben Sherman shirts, loafers or plains. I recall that people loved the heavy oxblood colour brogues, which were enlivened and deepened by applications of the right shoe polish. Mods also liked desert boots, which I don't remember skins wearing at all. Not so good for the kicking of heads, for which it needed to be thick leather. I can also clearly recall the sound they made, as many skins wore small iron Blakeys on the heels and the front of their shoes to stop the leather soles from wearing out so fast.

As a young kid, mod certainly influenced me. Especially the mod bands. I adored The Small Faces and thought Steve Marriott was practically the best thing I'd ever heard, so I had to showcase him in this book. It was important to me to mix fiction with factual events and people from that time. This book is set between late winter 1962 and late summer 1964, with a present day coda. Just over a year and a half, but so many tumultuous things happened. Apart from the John Profumo scandal and the fall of the British government, there was the mod scene, the assassination of JFK and the emergence and subsequent explosion of The Beatles. All of these events plus the arrival of ska, bluebeat, American soul and R&B music. Whew!

Many of the characters - like Christine Keeler, Lucky Gordon, Johnny Edgecombe, Georgie Fame, Ace Kefford, Trevor Burton - are real people. And there are some characters based on people I knew, such as Landy Gray. Landy was a West Indian boy who was my best friend for many years growing up in West London.

Paulette Harrison was a girl I fancied loads at school. Danny Healy was the name of another school friend. Neill Donnelly was a kid I disliked a lot at secondary modern and he became the rocker figure. Many of the others, like Karl Yelland, Eddie Emmons, Massini, Wirral, Hendry, Sales and so on, are concoctions of my imagination, but formed by paying careful attention to people I have met. Various episodes from my life have fuelled these characters in some manner or another.

The importance of amphetamines cannot be overemphasised in the mod scene. As a young kid, I discovered Philon and other speed pills very early on and this was the chemical beat all the mods were marching to. Speed was initially a revelation. When Landy and I first took it, at the age of 14 I believe, we trooped from Hanwell to

Harlesden and back in one night. We furiously put the world to rights and discovered that we had walked around ten miles, all the while chomping and talking and just speeding out of our heads. It was important for me to show how Spike comes a cropper through constant speed usage, as it can push people into semi-psychotic behaviour through constant use and abuse. Much of the mod violence will have been amphetamine charged. It was the same with the later punk scene, where cheap 'blues' and amphetamine sulphate were (mainly) the drugs of choice.

The mod scene was the first time working class youth had a voice. As someone who believes that most of the great bands, styles and trends have arisen from the street, it is fascinating to see that as soon as youth had the opportunity to shine, it did so, utterly and brilliantly.

Youth was not only displaying great taste in clothes, but also showing open hearts and ears for great American and Jamaican imported music, which was by then landing on our shores and becoming an integral part of the mod experience. This love of black music gave many bands their initial impetus: The Beatles, The Stones, The Small Faces, The Move, The Who and many more.

Living for Kicks was a great graphic novel to write and I hope you get caught up in the excitement and surreal freshness of a fleeting, long-vanished world that was the springboard for a seminal cultural explosion that continues to reverberate to this day.

Jim McCarthy
February 2016

Jim & Paulette

Jim & Landy changing from skins to a more soul-power-type dress and attitude.

Jim & Landy as skinheads.

In a poncey normal job, you'll be lucky to find twelve nicker a week in your pay packet. I give mum and dad 50 bob a week and that sorts out all the rent and meals and stuff.

Paulette, my bird, her mate Leslie Milligan, my best mates Danny Healy and Karl Yelland, they all wonder how I get my money.

My mum and dad can't work it out either.

How the fuck am I getting my dosh and maintaining my lifestyle?

Selling speed pills gives me that money, easy peasy, lemon squeezy.

Some Durophets, y'know, Black Bombers, or some Drinamyl, also known as Purple Hearts, mate.

Well handsome.

I'm seeing Paulette soon. I am in love with her and she is the original sweet sixteen. I know she worries a lot about me, y'know, about what I'm up to.

I think Paulette suspects the drugs thing. Good job she don't know, for sure 'cos I want to take it all a lot further than I have. She'd go completely fucking garrity.

I know she wants me to settle down. Get a job in an architects' office, if I could swing it. Y'know, the semi-detached out in Essex or in the East End. She's really got the Irish Catholic thing going as well. All that Catholic guilt. But I have got to get this MODerne thing up and running.

Oi, Spike! Where you gone, mate? Daydreaming about MODerne studios again?

That guy we heard about, knocking about in north London I think, was his name Joe Meek?

He has his own studio in Holloway Road where he records his acts.

Yeah Karl, he has that single out, 'Johnny Remember Me', and that 'Telstar' thing, that instrumental.

I didn't like them at all, but he got it going on his own, outside of the big record labels in London.

Someone said he's in Islington, wherever that is...

I wanna do what he's done, except bigger, better and much more mod, more hip.

Spike, I reckon this MODerne studio could really take off, mate.

It's there for the taking.

Cedar Club, Constitution Hill, Birmingham.

Mr Tooley please. Are you Bomber?

Maybe, who's asking?

I'm Spike Spellane, here to see Mr Tooley. Eddie Emmons sent me up from London.

You'll be Spike, Eddie's boy from London.

You're not one of those flash southern sods, are yer?

No Mr Tooley, I am a very respectful southern sod. I've brought up those goods that Mr Emmons wanted you to have personally delivered.

Alex's Pie Stand, Dudley Street.

ALEX

Late night, central Birmingham.

We'll see who I meet here... might as well meet some Birmingham faces if there are any around...

These two guys look really extra cool.

Hi, I'm up here from London.

I wondered what the music scene is like up here?

Wow! This guy almost looks like me! How bloody weird, he's almost a dead ringer.

Bloody hell! This guy almost looks like me! Is it my twin or summat?

I'm Spike Spellane from London, I'm about to set up a label and recording studio down there. What are you guys into?

My name's Trevor Burton. I come from Aston and oi'm just starting out playing guitar and singing. I'm getting a band together called The Everglades. Me an' Ace hang about The Beehive or The Whiskey A Go-Go above Chetwyns the tailors up here. You can get great clothes and also hear some good music upstairs.

And I'm Chris Kefford, but I'm also called Ace, Ace the face, mate! Me and Trev are looking to get a band started at some stage. I play bass and sing in The Shantelles with my uncles.

You guys look so young but you're getting things going up here, right?

There's a big scene happening up here but a lot of it is just local bands doing cover versions. One day me and Trev will break out with some new happening stuff.

Mission accomplished, Mr Emmons. Got it delivered to Mr Tooley, so I'm reporting back for further instructions.

Deptford High Street, south east London.

Well done, my son.

I'll be getting you readied up for the Soho business right sharpish.

I need you to meet a contact of mine in the Soho clubs. A right weasel I got here. He's called Lenny Wirral.

Come on in Lenny!

Look here, Spike, see this right forlorn tit here? This is Lenny Wirral. He's a right little rodent. A real dwarfish tosser but he knows every scumbag, he knows all the would-be gangsters and every soddin' miscreant in fucking Soho.

Eddie, is this the kid you were talking to me abaht?

Don't you, Lenny?

Lenny has his lugholes in all the right watering holes, in all the right places. He knows what is occurring and reports back to me, don't yer Lenny?

Yes Mr Emmons, you know I know, all the goss... all the main blag. All of what's occurring at street level.

Well son, here's something up front for the Soho business, some other bunce for the Birmingham run and some readies for you.

It's your bung, son.

That few bob'll keep you dry for a bit. I'll give you some bags with pills in too...

Thanks, Mr Emmons.

Yes, Spike mate. I'll show you how to work the club, the right places for everyone... how to set it up and where we will be serving up the pills.

That's it, Spike, let uncle Lenny show ya the ropes and then we'll be ready to start getting produce out to the punters.

There's just one big thorn in our side: a right entrenched fucker in Soho called Baldassar Massini.

His mob run some of the clubs from out of the Archway and Kentish Town areas of London.

They are Maltesers, know what I mean?

They are from Malta, like.

Maybe I can help Spike out here.

Get this all going faster, get on and do some dealing myself.

Make it a nice sideline and a nice earner too. I'm going to need some income myself soon.

See ya guys.

I'll see you next week in London for that movie and some business. Danny, remember we're taking Paulette and Leslie, alright?

Alright Spike, see you later boss.

See ya Spike.

Karl, let's take a ride out to the Mocha Bar in Ilford.

I need more stimulants in the form of a blast of coffee or sumthin'.

Let's hit the open road.

Ha ha ha, I'm still minging...

...these Black Bombers last for ages, mate.

Le Kilt Club, Soho, central London.

One of Baldassar Massini's many offices.

I perceive threat, I analyse threat and then I deal with threat.

I see that those Kray brothers from the East End have tried courting the US Mafia over here in central London. They want into the vice and gambling scene.

They should stay in their shithole club The Kentucky over in Stepney. We made sure that did not happen. Firmly and without too much fuss, we will fuck them off back to Vallance Road.

I am surrounded by enemies.

It has always been that way for us.

The police can be bought and paid off, so I don't have to worry about them...

... but the others? There is this scumbag Eddie Emmons, out of Deptford, a Godforsaken dump. He thinks he can come up here and work on my patch, come here and deal drugs in my domain...

I have my eyes and my ears all around...

I will always maintain and protect my assets.

The Mocha coffee bar, Ilford, east London/Essex borders

Fuck me, look over there. It's Neill Donnelly, all done up in leathers and what not.

What a prick! He was a year above us in school, d'ya remember the dozy bollocks, Karl?

Yeah, I remember him alright. A right flash bastard, always acting the tough guy. Looks like he's become a fucking grebo, a right greaser.

Oi Healy, you still hanging around that Leslie Milligan, hoping to get a sniff, you poor prat? Wouldn't mind a go at her myself!

Oi cunt, got any spare cash?

Why don't you go and sell your combined bumholes? You might both raise a thruppenny piece.

You pair of arse pirates, look at the state of ya! You daft pair of ponces.

He doesn't suspect me, does he?

OK, Danny, let Leslie up for air...

... you're going to suffocate her, mate...

I think we should get away for awhile and really talk about our future, Spike.

With my sister Maria dying so sudden, I feel very unsettled at the present...

Give me some time to get this new business going, then we can get away and really look at us, Paulette. That's what I want, honest.

Well, it's time for a friendly boost up.

We've been sitting in here for nearly three-and-a-half hours and now it's time to give it some.

Le Kilt club, Greek Street, Soho, London.

It's a bit middle class here. All French birds, right up their own arses, but I thought we could start off in here and then maybe take in the 'mingo later...

I love the music here, Paulette.

Let's get out and make some moves.

Here, Spike! Who's that guy over there? He's been staring at us.

Don't worry, Paulette, I know him... he's a geezer up from west London called Landy Gray.

Oi, Landy, come on over, mate. What's occurring?

The Flamingo club, 33 Wardour Street, Soho, London. Around midnight.

What's the scene like here, Landy?

It's the top, mate. Really great new import records brought in by the US air guys and a great new band just starting residency here tonight called Georgie Fame and the Blue Flames.

Listen, let your mate Danny and your two girls go get some drinks and dance on and we'll talk some business, OK?

Spike, I'd like to introduce you to a coupla movers around here.

First up, this is Aloysius Lucky Gordon...

Lucky, meet Spike Spellane.

Alright Lucky, nice to meet you.

Nice to be met, mon, how iz tings with you?

... and also Mr Johhny Edgecombe, Spike.

Hi Johnny, Lucky.

Well, I guess we have some speaking to do. Mr Emmons has told me about you guys...

The Flamingo, 1:30am.

Thanks!! That was 'Hit The Road Jack', a US hit for Mr Ray Charles! Hey everybody, great to be here tonight. Great to see all you US air force guys here tonight. It's just like playing a club in New York! Big shout out to our piano player, Psycho Gordon, whose brother Lucky is in the audience tonight...

We're doing two sets tonight, now and later at 4:00am.

Remember everybody, a big hand for Tubby Hayes, who played here earlier. Appearing here tomorrow night, with Jack Bruce and Ginger Baker, a great bass man and drummer, are The Johnny Birch Quartet.

We'll be doing alternate sets for you...

I'm flying off my head, Spike, and I'm loving this club.

We gotta come back here.

You keep on whizzing, Danny, 'cos this fucking place don't close till 6:00am, mate! We'll be back here next weekend to get the business going, OK!

By the way, where is Karl this weekend?

Karl is being grounded at the moment by his parents. He's complaining about having no dosh to spend as well.

Can't run his scooter, he was saying.

He said he might have to do some side work for that teacher guy O'Riordan from our school.

Or my ex-school...

I just got the fucking boot, they expelled me.

The Flamingo Club.

That next weekend, the beginning of the business rolled around...

... the end of the beginning...

Alright, so Johnny and Lucky are dealing from the front of the house and the door, keeping an eye on proceedings.

We're staying back in the club and will sell from near and around the bogs.

Anodder ting, Spike...

... that Lenny Wirral man, there's talk he's in the pockets of two local Soho detective bumba claats called Micky Hendry and Tony Sales, ya hear me?

Eddie Emmons told us to keep our eyes on this claat.

I'll be watching the fucker... he's watching every move I'm making.

He thinks he's the dog's nuts, but I ain't stupid.

OK chaps, let's make some money here.

I gotta call Sales and Hendry... those bastards never leave me alone.

They think I'm a grass. If Emmons finds out I'm giving them information, I'm fucking brown bread.

I can't ever be heard to be flapping my gums abaht anything notable to those two coppers.

Yeah, they're here now and they've started punting some smarties.

Yeah, Edgecombe and Lucky Gordon are in the frame too...

Yeah alright, I'll be around... you pair of prats...

Eddie Emmons called me, mon. He asked how tings were shaping.

I tol' him that everything is cool sir. The distribution is in place, now it's just the selling and there are some big orders to fill soon.

I feel a sense of threat coming from somewhere, but I don't know from who or what.

We've only bin at this five fucking minutes. Let's hope everything is cool, Landy...

I had anuther call from that prick friend of Spike's, Karl. How'd he get my fucking number? Maybe Healy senior fronted it to him...

He wants to talk and meet at Le Kilt.

Glad you could make it.

Look, Lenny, you know Spike is sorting it out at The Flamingo, waiting on orders to expand the business. Well, I need to make some cash urgently, so that I can survive myself and push some earnings towards Spike's studio set up at the same time.

Look son, you are steppin' into uncharted waters. I'll help you out this once, but after that you're on your own, get me?

An' keep your fucking mouth shut or you're going to end up a casualty. An' me, if you drag me into any of your shit.

Firstly, let's get some drinks in.

It's your round, mate.

I've already got a batch of pills sorted out.

They're here with me, so I can start knocking them out pronto.

So, get yourself some stuff sold here tonight, nice and easy like.

An' don't attract attention in here, this is a supposed Massini gang hangout.

That fucking Malteser bastard! Laying down the law to me. It's looking like a turf war is on the way...

Oi! Find out what's going on up there in Soho. Massini's bin on the phone... someone has been sussed out dealing on his patch.

I told Spike, Lenny and the other West Indian herberts that they were to stay off that one and concentrate on The Flamingo to begin with!

I can't afford a war against these Massini boys. They are too entrenched in Soho and can call on too many favours with Vice and the CID. They got too much protection.

The partially built MODerne studios, Manor Park, East London.

So Karl's parents and his teacher, John O'Riordan, haven't seen him since before the weekend?

Apparently he was seen dealing pills and in the company of Lenny Wirral at Le Kilt club... same time we was setting up operations at The Flamingo.

Lenny Wirral was, y'know, crucified. He was stone dead, nailed up in those garages in the back of Soho.

Someone has sent a fucking huge warning. It must be to do with Karl, Lenny or us.

What does it mean? So Karl was up there? I thought he was grounded. At home like, although I know he was really needing some money.

This is a right turnabout. Baldassar Massini musta done this.

He phoned me and said he was going to leave me a 'subtle' message, just last week.

Maltese prick!

It was horrible... he was nailed to the garage door and there was just that little card I showed you.

I want to see this mate of yours, Karl. You say you don't know where he is? Well, bloody well find him!

He must have heard or know something abaht alla this?

Have a look abaht the Soho parish. He might be hiding around there, daft as it sounds.

Hiding in plain sight, the silly cunt...

This is what you're going to do, sonny.

You are going to go to Le Kilt tonight sharpish and find out if any bastard knows anything about this Karl Yelland and where he's at.

Get moving! And we'll be watching you. Yelland must have something on Lenny Wirral and by definition Massini...

Alright, alright...

I'll keep it low profile... ask around, but nothing too obvious... see if anyone knows what Karl is doing. This is mental...

These two were outside the club.

They seem interested in me... following me... I don't like this.

Well, it's funny you say that, as we heard the weirdest thing from some of the ladies that frequent the streets here, where I preach, in my ordained fashion.

As God is my judge, we heard that a young man is working as a different version of himself, so to speak, in a strip club or clip joint somewhere behind Old Compton Street.

Sorry, hold up! Spike, look at this prick, what a herbert.

Did you injure your arms during the war, mate?

What the fuck... I know... you had that suit made to measure at Burton's... you fucking haddock!

Bollocks!

Well, Danny! As I was saying, this boy, who has made some drastic changes, is ensconced in the bosom or bosoms, so to speak, of some of our local ladies.

I could tell Vicky DeLampard and Lucky Diamonds that you are seeking information. They might need a little financial lubrication, though.

Please Tops... we need to find out what's going on... to make sure that Karl's safe and sort stuff out wiv his parents an' all that.

It got so bad for me, son, with drugs and booze, that I nearly topped myself... but the good Lord entered my heart and my world and now I am standing on top, so to speak.

Thanks Tops. What's with your name by the way?

Around the corner and another sub world of Soho. Old Compton Street, in fact... ladies of the night and day... strip clubs, clip joints... all human strife was here.

NON·STOP STRIPTEASE

SELF SERVI SHO

Here's the addy on the paper from Tops.

Let's jump in and talk to Vicky DeLampard and Lucky Diamonds... wot a weird pair a' names!

Think they call these gaffs walk ups... pay your money for a bunkup or a gum job.

Apparently Wirral told me all the prozzers were driven off the streets by the rozzers around here. Prozzers, rozzers, I like that... poetic, eh?

What the fuck are we getting into here, Spike?

This is a long way from Manor Park...

Georgie Fame and the Blue Flames were bedding in for the first of two hot sessions tonight at The Flamingo.

Yes Spike, they is complications, in that Christine Keeler, Lucky Gordon and Johnny Edgecombe triangle ting that Lenny Wirral spoke of...

God rest Wirral mon, that was a terrible ting too.

Landy, what the fuck else can go wrong?

It's too much, all this shit in the last few weeks.

Well, Keeler was buying some weed from Lucky, and she was dating himself too, for a moment. Johnny has heard this and is none too happy, mon... then Keeler breaks it off with Lucky... he goes fuckin' mad, mon, and held her hostage in a flat, wielding an axe and all kinds of ting.

....SWWWWWWITTTTTTT........

That was for Christine, you stupid ponce...

... wear it well and remember why...

This is another bloody nightmare!

I've got to a good stage with MODerne but need the recording console, which I can get second-hand if I can lay my hands on some more money.

No Karl, he's still missing.

Paulette is always on my case now... Danny is getting earache from Leslie, too...

... my mum and dad are giving me GBH of the earhole...

Emmons is totally pissed off with Edgecombe...

Ilford High Street.

Things need to quieten down at The Flamingo... time to get moving on the pills again.

Oi! Where's that fucker Danny Healy?

You're his mate, ain't ya? I seen ya!

Huh?

I'll be seeing you around, tosser, and your wanker mate Healy!

Edgware Road, London.

Johnny Edgecombe was a jilted and dangerously unsettled man...

Lucky Gordon has still bin threatening Christine.

He has a gun, too, a Luger me heard... she has finish with me... and wants it all over...

I hop a taxi and follow her to where she be...

She has gone here to see that guy Stephen Ward.

Wimpole Mews, December 1962.

Come out, Christine, I know you're in there, fuckin' claat.

Come out!!

Six random shots at Stephen Ward's door, shots that will echo deep... the downfall of a government...

Johnny, Emmons is getting right angry now.

Things have got to calm down pronto, before the whole Flamingo deal is blown out completely.

Edgecombe's court appearance made the front pages.

What's the connection here?

This seems close to the government... with this Edgecombe criminal in court.

The Telegraph

Look Christine, I am worried about that crazy bastard Gordon an' him doing a reprisal and ting. Help me wid a solicitah, so I can defend meself.

I am sorry about the shooting, but I really want you inna mi' life gal.

Why don't you piss off, Johnny. I'm sick of the both of you.

You pair of vicious, mad, controlling bastards... I am going to dob you into the courts right and proper.

Time slipped quietly and quickly into 1963... and it felt as if the whole world was starting to wake up. It was a very good time, with testosterone and oestrogen flying and merging... escaping the dreary days we had lived through. It was a time to be one hundred percent alive...

Hiya Tops. Hi Storey. How's things? What you guys listening to on this cold Soho afternoon?

We're listening to a new group called The Beatles.

It's not as good as real mod stuff, Tops. D'ya reckon they'll catch on? What's the ear'ole on Karl, or should I say Tracey? Any more news?

He has been seen again by us around Old Compton Street, as well as round the back of Shaftesbury Avenue, but always seems to vanish into thin air... like a bloody wraith.

All quiet on the 1963 front... or so we all thought.

Turn on Thank Your Lucky Stars on the old telly.

What's all this about, then?

PLEASE, PLEASE ME, OH YEEEAAAAHHHHH...

The Ace Cafe, North Circular Road, London. Neill Donnelly was talking with another rocker.

Yeah, I saw them again in Ilford, and the one who seems like the main one in Ilford High Street the week before that... there's some talk of some major bundles coming up soon.

I reckon we could do 'em all, under cover of alla that aggro.

The Spellane home, Ilford. It is said everyone remembers where they were... exactly.

It has been announced that President John Fitzgerald Kennedy has been fatally shot in Dallas, Texas. He died at Parkland Hospital in Dallas at 1:00pm American time.

The historic date is 22nd November 1963.

Jasus, that's the beginning of the bleddy end for all of us... if they can shoot the President in broad daylight!

Maybe Dad's right. There has been a sort of shift in the world.

I will certainly remember this moment... a chilling minute...

Soho... the need for money was still increasingly paramount... as the winter of 1963 draws in ever colder...

I'm going to need to bring in a lot more money really quick if we are going to survive alla this shit that has rained down on us.

Don't wanna end up with just this thruppenny bit.

I don't believe this... Keeler is all over the paper... so she has had an affair with that minister John Profumo.

How many geezers has she bloody well got?

I guess with all the other stuff that's happened, Lucky Gordon and Johnny Edgecombe are fucking involved in this shit too. Fuck me, what a major fiasco.

Funny how the streets, in their own way, could take down a government... from Soho to the corridors of power... the ripples spread outwards...

A government in complete tatters... the Conservative Prime Minister of Great Britain, Harold MacMillan, was forced to resign... with Lucky Gordon and Johnny Edgecombe as bit players.

Christine Keeler got done for perjury. She withdrew her charges against Lucky Gordon and got a nine month sentence for her troubles... and for the first time, we all got a real look-see at the ruling class in Britain.

I gotta band called The Moments as well as that... we done a demo, which could get off the ground.

Spike, mate, all around this street there are loads of charvers looking for songs... right new stuff, like.

This is Duffy... meet Spike Spellane.

Stevie's right.

I recorded a cover of The Beatles' 'I Saw Her Standing There', with some top London guys... Graham Bond, Ginger Baker and a bass man called Jack Bruce...

I hope this is a way in. Then it's going to be my stuff, I hope. Stevie's done a cover too, right? Cliff Richard's 'Move It'.

Duffy, I'm setting up a studio in Manor Park, the East End like... looking for new talent, mod or ska, R&B, y'know.

1963 swiftly scrambled into 1964. They say 1963 was the year that the old England died...

MODerne studios

What a year!

I can't really get to grips with all that's happened.

Yeah, what about those Great Train Robbers an' all, Spike, do you reckon they'll get nabbed by the rozzers?

Gerrard Street, Soho, London. A meeting outside Ronnie Scott's basement jazz club.

Well Tops, you had a recent sighting of Karl?

Yes, definitely this time.

We saw him enter and leave a doorway to... we think the clip joint at the end of Gerrard Street, just down the way here... just on the edge of Chinatown.

This looks pretty secret, Danny.

No sign, no nothing.

Here, hold up!

Is that you, Karl, is that y..?

Clacton, an Essex seaside resort.

The coldest Easter Bank Holiday since 1863.

Monday, March 30th 1964.

Some of us had arrived already, but there was nothing happening. Well, not yet, anyway...

Off you go, sonny Jim!

We don't want your sort in our resort, out here to cause bloody trouble.

Call this a resort?

You're jokin', ain't ya?

I've been in better mortuaries than this... what a fucking dump!

An' my name ain't Jim, you prize prat!

Looks like things just took a turn for the better.

At least we can warm up a bit... it's bloody brass monkeys, it's freezing down here... at least I'm whizzed right up.

Things simmered down, but not for long.

Whitsun Bank Holiday, 19th and 20th May 1964

Oi, Danny, where are ya, mate?

I heard that Donnelly grebo is also down here somewhere amongst all this.

Magistrates in Margate jailed four young men and imposed fines totalling £1,900 on 36 people.

We fought the bloody Nazis for these bloody hooligans.

Ninety-seven arrests in our lovely, genteel town of Margate already.

What is the world coming to when we can't walk down our own streets in peace?

There were a good few spots of bother along the coast in Southend, Bournemouth, Brighton and Broadstairs, as well as a Whitsun return to Margate.

Let's have some here...

...get these greaser bastards, c'mon!

Spike, if you see Neill Donnelly, point the tosser out to me. I'm going to have him twice.

Definitely Danny. He might be about. I heard there was a lot of rockers over in Brighton as well...

We fought the law... seems a bit like equals to me... time for a break in the proceedings...

Just like being on 'oliday, init Spike?

Except here you get a nice bit of aggro thrown in for free, too.

There were a good few bundles all over: Bognor, Southend... forty arrests in Bournemouth... and back in Margate, Dr George Simpson doled out summary fines and punishments to the arrested mods.

It is not likely that the air of this town has ever been so polluted by hordes of hooligans, male and female, such as we have seen this weekend, and of whom you are an example. These long haired, mentally unstable, petty little sawdust Caesars seem to only find courage like rats by hunting in packs. We shall discourage you and other thugs of your kind who are infected with this vicious virus. Margate will not tolerate louts like you.

In Brighton, on the Sussex coast, mods had gathered in even larger throngs to do battle with their enemy.

May 18th 1964. Seventeen year-old Barry Prior took a walk.

What a weekend! It's a bloody lot different to the time The Who played down here about a month ago.

At 7:00am next morning, Barry's mates found him lying at the bottom of Telscombe Cliffs, Saltdean, Sussex.

No one saw nothing during the night and there was no screams or nothing.

Let's get over to those houses and get someone to get the police down here straight away!

Barry musta just fell... This is bloody horrible!

In Brighton, mods congregated around Marine Parade and brought that part of town to a standstill.

The mod pack started to bay for some biker blood.

Let's get this bastard and his mate!

You are to fall back and start to form orderly lines.

Get off the streets and back onto the pavements.

At approximately 1:00pm that afternoon there was a good response to that request.

Margate was left to its own devices after a two day violence binge that took the British public by surprise.

Time to leave Margate for good, I think.

What a God-forsaken dump. We've left our mark here, though.

Spike, I called mum up earlier.

She said things were kicking off in Brighton and other seaside towns too.

Three thousand had assembled in front of The Palace Pier in Brighton... and streamed towards Madeira Drive and then on to the Aquarium Sun Terrace.

These bastards are gonna kill us, throwing those deckchairs.

Let's try and get out of here.

There were 150 policemen on hand, led by PC Ken Thomas on a stalwart horse called Kim.

Kim, you might be twelve years old, but you can rout these bloody bastards any day.

Alright, start to disperse!! Do you hear me? Start to disperse at once!!

As the temperatures plummeted from the day before...
...the tempers and anger soared.

Here, have this... and put yourselves in it afterwards, you rubbish wankers!

The scene was changing... getting angrier and more violent.

You rockers are just all third class tickets!

No quarter was given... or expected...

Keep an eye out for that Danny Healy wanker and 'is poncey mate... that blonde bastard.

The holidaymakers were asleep to the world... until this agitated, speed-driven swarm broke up their reveries.

'Ere, Albert, what's all that noise about?

It's coming from up top on the promenade.

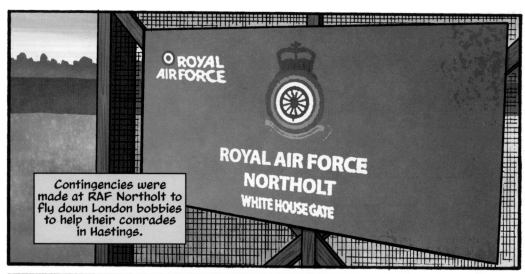

Contingencies were made at RAF Northolt to fly down London bobbies to help their comrades in Hastings.

The police got the word to go...

They were a new sort of 'flying squad' in the air.

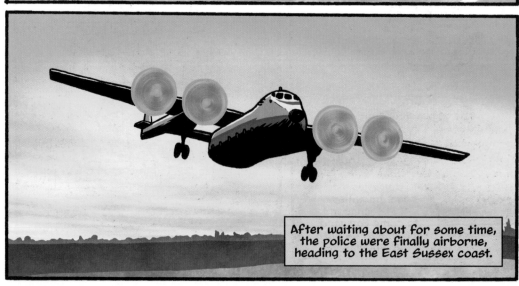

After waiting about for some time, the police were finally airborne, heading to the East Sussex coast.

A fatality was also recorded...

Is that someone larking about?

Here, what's that out in the sea?

Oi! Are you alright out there?

Young James Smart, aged 14 years old, was found drowned on the Hastings shore that day in August...

We are looking for a young man, a rocker from Eastbourne called Robert Baird, who gave an eyewitness report stating that he saw James being thrown over the East Cliff.

We appeal to this teenager to come forward and assist us with our enquiries.

Did he fall 200 feet over the East Cliff near Hastings Old Town or was he pushed?

D'ya reckon a rocker pushed him over the edge?

That's right bloody weird... none of theirs has got killed, like.

Hastings, the fighting continued... the skies darkened...

I've lost Danny and me mates and nearly got cornered... I'm going to head for the Old Town in Hastings.

Past Claremont to the seafront... past Peter Jackson's shop that sold good mod clobber...

Sorry mates, where are you guys from?

A geographical surprise...

We are called Som and Viking and we are mods and we here from Thailand as the students here in this town.

Meet you happy and very pleased that we are.

I never met no one from Thailand before.

Come on then, lads. I'm trying to find my mate near the Old Town down by the cliffs and the fishing huts.

Police were trying to obtain shoelaces from the mods and rockers to stop all the kickings being handed out.

This is fucking ridiculous, officer.

How the fuck am I supposed to defend myself against these greaser barbarians?

Desert boots made a great soft noise as you strode purposefully into your new day... everything else fell away as you walked with meaning and attitude... the noise they made was that of considered style.

God!

It's Neill Donnelly and that crew from the Ace Cafe in London.

I'm brown bread if he sees me...

Later on 70 arrests were recorded in Hastings... due to the running violence...

I'm almost down to the Old Town fishermen's huts.

That was me and Danny's fall back point to meet... if we got lost...

The day drew inwards...

A moment of peace, perhaps?

Remember me, you cunt?

I can't find Healy anywhere, so you'll have to do, you bastard.

Or perhaps not...

Hammer House, 113-117 Wardour Street, Soho.

These days...

Enter the doors and walk down the corridors...

MODerne
Film Productions Ltd

Yes, yes...

I got that...

...right away!

We can deliver those by next week.

Another film production company struggling to survive in London's Soho...

Yes, the production is finished and all the post-production is completed as of this week.

...but thriving in its own micro-budget fashion.

Hey, Spike!

A call for you on line one... thanks.

SPIKE SPELLANE

A new film production has been completed.

After MODerne collapsed back in the mod days, it's great to be making a series of low-budget horror feature crud.

Keeps me off the streets... I think back a lot about what coulda been an' what was... and is...

Making low-budget horror films for the straight-to-DVD and download audience.

Emmons bought it years back in Deptford and no one got brought to justice, none of the Massini crew got done, that's for sure.

The coppers didn't care... another dead criminal scumbag as far as... along with Lenny Wirral, poor fucker.

Camp ain't the word for this stuff.

This is my tribute, if ya like, to Karl.

He never was found... broke our hearts, but he just vanished... perhaps dead...

We'll never know, none of us...

Rodeo Vampires And The Necking Crew ... a gay vampire movie, wouldja believe? This camp shit is my way of saying hallo and goodbye to Karl.

Scars heal but heart wounds take a lot longer...

Danny did time, the silly sod.

He's out and married now... same as Paulette... we don't talk no more... tried, but no... there's no going back, is there?

Donnelly got killed in a bike crash. Who cares?

Not me.

It all seems so long ago, but sort of like yesterday...

That scar is my mod tattoo, mate, not some fucking Chinese hieroglyphics.

Not a tattoo of some new age bollocks or Eastern mandala type shit. Not like all that flaky ink some tossers have on 'em these days.

That was my earnings for being in them fucking wars... my reminder...

the cast of **Living for Kicks**

Spike Spellane: A 16-year-old good-looking alpha male. Our story's main protagonist, anti-hero and mod survivor.

Karl Yelland: Spike's good friend, a pretty boy, with a secret and confused gay sexuality. This leads to his eventual disappearance.

Danny Healy: Spike's good friend, also 16 years of age. Shorter, dark haired, pugilistic, loyal, temperamental and very hotheaded.

Paulette Harrison: Spike's girlfriend, stable, cool, sexual, alluring, determined. Her need for early stability and Spike's lies drive the lovelorn couple apart.

Leslie Milligan: Danny Healy's girlfriend, faithful, sexual, friendship-orientated. She is Paulette's best friend and they form a mod foursome.

Neill Donnelly: A rocker in his late twenties, who is the main biker figure in the story. Has a violence-based vendetta against Danny Healy in particular.

John O'Riordan: Karl Yelland's art teacher, a young, foppish, trendy and secretly gay man. An extra curricular visit from Karl will set a chain of events in motion.

Eddie Emmons: Deptford-based gangster trying to gain ground in the Soho drugs and extortion rackets. Uses Spike to head up a speed-dealing team in Soho.

Lenny Wirral: Eddie Emmons' lackey and general dogsbody. The hapless and seedy gangster Wirral becomes a target in a horrific Soho killing. Knows where all the bodies are buried.

Baldassar Massini: Maltese gang crime head, runs Soho crime, silently and ruthlessly. A more traditional and efficient old-school gangster.

Colin Tooley: Birmingham and Midlands-based crime boss. Has links to Eddie Emmons and runs various drug and other crime rackets from the Constitution Hill area of Birmingham.

Johnny Edgecombe (real-life character): West Indian hustler, mover and shaker and face about Soho. Briefly Christine Keeler's boyfriend and also a habitué of the feted Flamingo Club. Involved in the infamous Profumo affair. Died aged 77 in 2010.

Landy Gray: Young West Indian boy, who wears a trademark pork pie hat. Landy is a young scenester with a humorous and adaptable personality.

Lucky Gordon (real-life character): West Indian with an unstable mien, a hustler, who briefly dates and also attempts to kill Christine Keeler. Peripherally involved in the infamous Profumo affair.

Psycho Gordon (real-life character): Piano-playing brother of Lucky Gordon, who also hung out at The Flamingo. He played and sat in with Georgie Fame And The Blue Flames.

Stevie Marriott (real-life character): Original face and scene maker. Went on to lead the glorious Small Faces. An original and totally unique talent. Died in an Essex house fire in 1991.

 Christine Keeler (real-life character): Call girl. Sexually alluring, she became embroiled in the infamous John Profumo scandal that brought down the Harold Macmillan government of the day.

 Micky Hendry: Vice Squad undercover and plainclothes copper on the make. Machievellian, scheming and totally underhanded.

 Tony Sales: Vice Squad plainclothes copper. Sly, nefarious, shifty and nasty. In professional and personal competition with Micky Hendry.

 Lucky Diamonds: A young man in his late twenties, very sexualized. A cross-dressing and extremely camp fantasist.

 Vicky DeLampard: A beautiful female stripper in her early twenties. Unsure, troubled, social, tempestuous.

 Tops Henderson: Funny, stand-alone, Christian and God fearing. Tops was a Soho based street-style preacher.

 Sometime Storey: Hanger-on and friend of Tops Henderson. He is young and nerdy with learning difficulties.

 Georgie Fame (real-life character): Renowned Hammond B3 keyboardist and a young hipster in the Soho scene. Led the popular band The Blue Flames with a (now) legendary late-night weekend residency at The Flamingo Club.

 Speedy Acquaye (real-life character): Georgie Fame's exotic Ghanaian conga drummer, an early proponent of Soho-based worldbeat and an unusual musical sight in the early 1960s.

 John McLaughlin (real-life character): Superb guitarist who went on to form The Mahavishnu Orchestra and other lightning-fast guitar-based jazz fusion ensembles. He was also a member of Georgie Fame's band.

 Duffy Power (real-life character): Soulful singer and songwriter who never quite made the upper echelons of the music business. Revered by other musicians in his day. Died in 2014.

 Ace Kefford (real-life character): A young and up-and-coming face on the early sixties Birmingham scene, he formed The Move. The group were infamously sued by Harold Wilson, the British Prime Minister, in 1967. Ace cracked up after bad drug experiences and now lives in Leamington Spa.

 Trevor Burton (real-life character): Formed The Move with Ace Kefford, as two young upstart mods. Burton was a talented and rebelliously fiery musician. Still playing the Midland blues clubs circuit.

mods slang **glossary**

Addy: Address.

Aggro: Aggravation or violence.

Arse pirate: A homosexual.

Barnet: Hair or hairstyle.

Bender: A homosexual.

Bird: Girl or young woman, girlfriend.

Black Bombers: Amphetamines, time release pills and powerful. Branded as Philon.

Blag: To obtain by dodgy means.

Bleddy: Irish for bloody.

Blood claat: A blood cloth/sanitary towel used as a Jamaican derogatory term. Variation on bumba claat.

Boat race: Rhyming slang for face.

Bob: Term for a shilling used in old pre-decimal UK currency (what would be 5p in today's currency).

Bogs: Toilets.

Bollocks: Testicles, balls or sometimes knackers.

Boost: To take some speed.

Brass: From brass nail, aka tail. A whore. A call girl.

Brass monkeys: Really cold, freezing.

Breadbasket: Head or noggin.

Brown bread: Rhyming slang for dead.

Bumba claat: A blood cloth/sanitary towel used as a Jamaican derogatory term. An ass wipe.

Bunce: Money, a bundle of money.

Bung: Receive some money in a dodgy fashion. A bribe.

Bunkup: Sex usually in the missionary position.

Buzzing: Speeding or high on speed or other drugs.

Bwoy: Jamaican term for man or boy.

Chaps: One of the men.

Charver: A dodgy/nasty geezer or woman.

Choice: Variation on tasty, very appropriate.

Clobber: Clothes, nice threads.

Cough: To talk, spill the beans, to tell the truth.

Crud: Rubbish, crap, low-level output.

Dob: To turn someone into the police.

Dog's nuts: The dog's bollocks, aka the very best.

Face: Noted hip individual in their locale.

Fecking: Irish for fucking.

Firm: A local gang on your manor

Flakey ink: Crappy or badly done tattoos.

Flash: Sharply dressed, up front and very showy.

Foggy: A kind of thick smog of pollution prevalent in UK cities in the 1960s.

Garrity: Going absolutely mental.

Geezer: One of the lads. One of the chaps. A righteous man. The American equivalent would be dude.

Grass: To fit up, to inform on someone.

Greaser: Biker.

Grebo: Derogatory term for a biker.

Grub: Food.

Guineas: Old pre-decimal money worth twenty-one shillings (or £1.05 in today's currency).

Haddock: Useless pratt or loser.

Handsome: Spot on.

Herberts: Hooligans or idiotic losers who get everything wrong.

Keep schtum: Keep your mouth firmly shut; to say nothing.

Larking about: Fooling or messing about.

Lugholes: Ears or earholes.

Maltesers: Derogatory term used by Eddie Emmons for Maltese people.

Minging: Out of one's head, speeding. Unsavoury or smelly.

Mingo: Abbreviated term for The Flamingo Club.

Miscreant: Dodgy, a law breaker.

Mon: Jamaican term for man.

Monkey's uncle: Amazement and surprise (not like "Couldn't give a monkeys").

Mush: Mate or good friend.

Neck: Swallow it down.

Occurring: Happening.

Pillock: An inept idiot, a total fool.

Ponce: Someone always on the take. Poser or fey wannabe.

Poncey: Frilly and useless, not worth it. Pretentious.

Pong: A rank smell.

Prat: Idiotic person, hapless idiot.

Prick: A worthless dickhead, a constant irritant socially.

Pronto: Urgent, as in NOW!

Prozzers: Prostitutes.

Purple Hearts: Amphetamines, aka speed. Branded as Dexamyl.

Rass: A Jamaican derogatory term for arse. Shortened version of rass claat.

Readies: Money in your hand.

Rozzers: Police.

Sah: Jamaican term for man.

Scarper: Run off very fast, to flee the scene.

Serving up: Selling drugs.

Shag bandy: Bow legged from too much sex.

Sharpish: On the double, to get it done quick.

Slag: A whore, a lowlife.

Smarties: Drugs of various kinds.

Snitch: A grass, a stool pigeon in American terms.

Sods: Idiots, a light expression.

Soppy: Soft, wet, feeble and completely prat-like.

Spazzy: Hyper or manic, an old-time and pre-PC expression.

Spielers: Glib talk, also a secret drinking den.

Tasty: Nice, cool, very appealing.

Third class tickets: Cheap and scruffy.

Thruppenny bit: A threepenny piece, also rhyming slang for tits.

Ting: Jamaican term for thing.

Toerag: A complete turd, a snivelling wretch of a person.

Ton: A hundred pounds.

Tosser: Also known as wanker or puller, a masturbator.

Tranny: Transvestite.

Wanker: Also known as a tosser, a puller, a masturbator.

Weasel: A rodent, a snivelling person.

Whizz: Speed.

Whoor: Irish for whore.

Living for Kicks gallery

Over the past few years, my work has become increasingly more cartoony, for lack of a better term. Looking at these sketches now that the book is done, I can see that I was trying to force my style to be a tad more realistic while retaining the cartoony aspects which come more naturally.

The final head sketches of a young Spike Spellane and his aged counterpart look foreign to me. Not my style at all. The interior pages of this book are evidence of the struggle, and eventual compromise, between what normally comes out of the end of my pencil and what was probably more appropriate for this book. I learned a lot making the pages and I hope the end result does justice to Jim's words.

SPIKE

RUBBISH!

Jim McCarthy

Living For Kicks is Jim's first original graphic novel for Omnibus Press, following his successful series of music biographies, which includes *Reckless Life: The Guns N' Roses Graphic* and *Metallica: Nothing Else Matters*. Among Jim's other titles are *Gabba Gabba Hey: The Graphic Story of the Ramones*, *Neverland: The Life And Death Of Michael Jackson*, three Bad Company paperback collections, *Godspeed: The Kurt Cobain Graphic*, *Death Rap: Tupac Shakur*, *Eminem: In My Skin*, *How To Draw Monsters For Kids* and *The Sex Pistols Graphic*.

Jim's first book, *Voices Of Latin Rock*, was published by Hal Leonard in North America and was the first in-depth examination of Santana, Latin rock culture and the Mission District of San Francisco, the area where this nascent political and musical art form emerged.

Jim's books have been translated and published in numerous foreign rights countries, including Russia, Czechoslovakia, Spain, Norway, Italy, Poland, France, Croatia, Germany and Japan.

www.jimmccarthy.co.uk

Kevin Cross

San Francisco Bay Area native Kevin Cross is currently living in Portland, Oregon with his rad daughter. He has been playing guitar, and occasionally screaming, in hardcore punk bands for over 30 years. Most notably Big Rig (Lookout! Records), The Nerve Agents (Revelation Records), and Pitch Black (Lookout! Records and Revelation Records).

Coupled with the creativity of the punk rock scene and his disdain for day jobs, Kevin stepped onto the path towards a career as an illustrator and cartoonist just over 15 years ago. He has undertaken a wide variety of work, including skateboard graphics, children's books, comics and storyboarding, to name just a few.

When he's not fighting the establishment through his music or making pictures for cash, Kevin stays up later than everyone else to work on his passion comic book project, *The Monkey Mod & Friends Show*. Additionally, Kevin likes to destroy his body skateboarding and enjoys a nice piece of lemon meringue pie.

www.kevincross.net